Orange Peel Porn

The ultimate self-mastery, manifestation guide.

Mychael T Renn

"The zest of life comes not from avoiding the bitter, but from embracing it fully"

Mychael T Renn

Contents

Dedication

To the seekers and the dreamers, who yearn to peel away the mundane to reveal the extraordinary within. May this book serve as your guide in the audacious journey of self-discovery and mastery, and may you find the courage to manifest a life as vibrant and daring as you dare to dream.

Welcome to Your Transformation Toolkit

Buckle up, brave soul! This isn't just another trot down self-help lane; you're about to dive into "Orange Peel Porn: The Ultimate Self-Mastery Manifestation Guide." This book isn't a passive read; it's an active journey into the very fabric of your being. You're holding a toolkit that could dismantle the predictable, comfortable patterns of your past and unlock a life you didn't realize you could have.

Why "Orange Peel Porn "?

Curious about the title? It does encourage a double-take, doesn't it? "Orange Peel Porn" isn't just about the tantalizing thrill of uncovering what lies beneath. It's about delving deep and revealing the essence of your fullest potential. We're not merely scratching the surface with timid pokes; we're boldly stripping back the layers, unleashing a spray of zest that will shock your ordinary into the extraordinary. This book is your guide to squeezing every drop of greatness from the seemingly mundane, transforming the everyday into a vibrant spectacle of self-discovery.

And "porn"? Because this is about the joy, the pleasure, the downright indulgence of discovering and mastering the depths of your own psyche. We're exploring every hidden corner of your mind, those places you've neglected or never dared to venture.

Before "Orange Peel Porn" found its unusual title, it was a labor of love, but titleless nonetheless. I spent over a year compiling insights, strategies, and personal anecdotes, meticulously crafting a guide that was bursting with transformative ideas yet hadn't found its voice. Then, fate stepped in through a vivid dream where I was publishing an ad for a magazine called "Orange Peel Porn." I saw the cover so clearly, and upon waking, I knew it was the perfect title. It was as if the book itself had chosen its identity, signaling it was ready to meet the world and squirt a blast of full potential right in the eye of mediocrity.

This Isn't Your Friend's Self-Help Book

Throw out any notions of conventional, run-of-the-mill self-help advice. What you're holding in your hands is something entirely different. "Orange Peel Porn" is not just a guide; it's a manifesto for radical change, blending diverse philosophies into a potent concoction that's as provocative as it is transformative.

Let me tell you a bit about the catalyst for this book. At 40, I was a boilermaker and had been for 16 years. It was a job that filled my pockets but emptied my spirit. Jim Rohn once said, "Don't ask yourself what you're getting from your job; ask yourself what you're becoming there." Well, what I was becoming was not who I wanted to be. I made the bold decision to stop evaluating my life based on who I had been and started shaping it based on what I could become.

So, I took the plunge—I quit my job, sold my house, and moved away from everything familiar to start fresh with the practices I share in this book. Fast forward three years, and I'm not just surviving; I'm thriving as a successful author with 3 books gracing shelves worldwide.

This book is for anyone who's ever felt like they were stuck on autopilot, living a life dictated by routines and societal expectations. It's for those ready to question not just the path they're on but also the person they've become along the way. If you're ready to shake up your life, embrace the known unknowns, and step away from a predictable past, then "Orange Peel Porn" is your gateway to a new beginning.

What's Inside?

Inside, you'll find a dynamic collection of tools, stories, and exercises that do more than just instruct—they transform. Each chapter is a meticulously crafted layer to peel back, designed to teach you how to quiet the noise, amplify your true desires, and manifest the life you've secretly dreamed of. From mastering mindfulness to hacking your brain's reward system, we've laid out everything you need to start living not just differently, but vibrantly.

Transformative Tools and Practical Exercises:

This guide is packed with practical tools that make abstract concepts tangible. You'll learn to master your environment, align your actions with your aspirations, and reshape your life through disciplined speech. Every exercise is an opportunity to reflect, adjust, and advance on your journey to self-mastery.

Innovative Worksheets:

To enhance your interactive learning experience, the book includes carefully designed worksheets in the back. These worksheets are concise and clear, providing structured templates to help you:

- Life Scripting made easy

- Organize and clean your living and working spaces for clarity and focus.
- Align daily actions with your long-term goals.
- Master the discipline of speech to positively influence your relationships and self-perception.
- Craft and recite powerful daily affirmations to reshape your reality.

Ready to Start Peeling?

If you've been waiting for a sign to take control of your life, consider this it. Prepare for laughs, lightbulb moments, and maybe even a little troublemaking. It's time to peel back the layers, discover your deepest desires, and have a blast doing it. Let's make this journey unforgettable.

"Yesterday I was clever, so I wanted to change the world. Today I am wise, so I am changing myself." - ***Rumi***

Chapter 1: Your Body, Your Subconscious

The Great Reveal: Your Body Is Your Subconscious

Welcome to the big reveal where we decode the mystery: Your body is not just a vehicle for your existence; it *is* literally your subconscious mind. Picture this: every beat of your heart, every healing cell, and even your reflexes are your subconscious pulling the strings behind the curtain without needing a conscious cue from you.

Here's the fun twist—your body acts out every command your subconscious throws down, from jerking your hand away from a hot surface to pumping adrenaline when you watch a thriller. These aren't just physiological responses; they're your subconscious mind dictating the script of your physical responses.

Now, let's get real: if your body is a reflection of your subconscious, what does being out of shape say about your inner thoughts? Think about it. The rich, the famous, and the go-getters—they usually sport health like it's part of their success uniform. It's no coincidence. It's their subconscious aligning with a mindset of vitality, success, and action.

"Who looks outside, dreams; who looks inside, awakes." –
Carl Jung

What Does Your Body Say About Your Mind?

If your subconscious were a garden, would it be full of weeds or flourishing with health? Your physical state—yes, whether you're fit, fatigued, or frazzled—is a direct reflection of the mental and emotional seeds you plant. An unhealthy body often mirrors a cluttered, neglected subconscious mind. It's time to ask yourself: Do I have a beautiful mind that nourishes a beautiful body?

This isn't about shaming the shape you're in; it's about realizing the power you hold to mold that shape. Your body is your subconscious made visible. Let that sink in. What you see in the mirror is your inner beliefs and scripts flexing in the physical world.

Turning the Subconscious into a Superpower

Knowing that your body is your subconscious, you wield the power to reshape both. It's like having the ultimate cheat code to life. Want to change your physical health? Start with the health of your thoughts. Cultivate a garden of positive, affirming beliefs, and watch as your body begins to reflect these with vitality and strength.

We're not just talking about thin equals win; we're talking health, energy, and vibrancy—whatever that looks like for you. Transforming your body by transforming your mind is the ultimate act of taking control of the subconscious narrative.

Manifesting Mastery: Own Your Reality

We'll dive deep into how to align your thoughts to not only heal but empower your body. Imagine programming your subconscious with such mastery that good health and energy are just natural reflections of your mental state. This chapter sets the stage for rewriting your physical script with every thought you choose.

Are you ready to join the ranks of those who not only know their power but live it? Let's peel back the layers of mundane existence with "Orange Peel Porn" and reveal the extraordinary power within you. It's time to get down with OPP—aligning your Outer Physical Presence with your Powerful Potential. Let's make this journey unforgettable, not just in how you think, but in how you live, look, and love.

Because if not now, when?

Urges vs. Desires: Who's Really in Charge?

The Tyranny of Urges

Urges are like unruly children of your subconscious, demanding immediate attention and gratification without considering the consequences. They hijack your body's action systems, making you reach for that extra slice of cake or scroll through social media aimlessly. However, when you recognize that these urges are just surface expressions of a deeper subconscious content, you can begin to take back control. By addressing urges directly, you teach your body—a manifestation of your subconscious mind—to adhere to the discipline of your conscious will. This mastery over urges is not just about denying yourself pleasures but about redirecting your energy towards more fulfilling and intentional actions.

Overcoming Laziness: The CEO of Your Subconscious

If you aim to be the CEO of your subconscious, mastering your environment is non-negotiable. Consider this: how can you expect to run a successful company if you can't even keep your garage clean? Every aspect of your surroundings is a reflection of your internal state. A cluttered, neglected garage is not just a mess; it's a manifestation of procrastination and disorganization in your subconscious.

Let's tackle laziness head-on. It's comfortable to overlook the small chores and the creeping disorder, but true self-mastery requires conquering these everyday challenges. Laziness isn't just about being idle; it's an active choice to ignore the things that need attention. And just as a CEO cannot afford to ignore the small details of their company, you cannot afford to overlook the details of your life.

Tip

Start Small

Begin with manageable tasks that you've been avoiding. Clean that garage, organize your desk, or sort out your emails. Small victories pave the way for bigger challenges.

Mastering the Masturbatory Muse: Why Keep Playing Solo?

Here's the lowdown: masturbating is like your body throwing a party when your mind's not home. Sure, it feels like seizing the moment, but really, it's just your primal urges crashing the brain's strategic planning session. We're here to master the subconscious, right? That means teaching your body to march to the beat of your long-term desires, not just dance to the quick pulse of immediate gratification.

So, next time your lower regions send out a party invite, RSVP with a 'no thanks, I'm busy building empires'. Turn those urges into energy for projects that pack a real punch. Remember, every time you choose not to go down the solo path, you're one step closer to becoming the master of your own domain. And isn't ruling an empire a lot more exhilarating than just playing with the scepter?

Redefining Fun: The Joy of Self-Mastery

Who says self-control can't be exhilarating? Redefining fun to include the joy of self-mastery transforms what could be a mundane or strenuous process into an engaging game of personal betterment. Each act of resistance against an urge strengthens your subconscious alignment with your conscious goals, turning discipline into a thrilling challenge. This is about enjoying the process of becoming the best version of yourself, celebrating each victory over a previously irresistible urge as a step towards mastering your own fate.

Embrace Your True Desires

True desires go beyond fleeting urges; they are profound yearnings that align with your deepest values and your true purpose. Unlike the impulsive wants that flash and fade, true desires are the calls of a well-aligned subconscious that echo through your body, seeking realization in the physical world. When you start to listen to these deeper calls and align your actions accordingly, you harness the full power of your subconscious—not just as a repository of urges but as a wellspring of aspiration. Embracing these true desires and allowing them to guide your actions is the ultimate form of manifestation, as it ensures that both your inner self and outer actions are in perfect harmony, paving the way for a fulfilled and purpose-driven life.

In this dance of urges versus desires, understanding that your body is your subconscious allows you to see the physical manifestations of internal conflicts and harmonies. By choosing to act on your true desires and control your urges, you're not just deciding what to do; you're deciding who you want to be. The power of manifestation lies not in wishful thinking but in deliberate action aligned with profound personal truth. Are you ready to take charge and let your true desires lead the way?

Snickers vs. Dream Partner

Let's talk choices: A Snickers bar or your dream partner? Back in the day, I really thought those Snickers bars were what I needed to get through. But let's be honest—they were just quick fixes, little sugar rushes that never truly satisfied. When I started trading those temporary fixes for consistent, healthier habits, it wasn't just my waistline that saw the benefits—it was my whole life.

Choosing fitness and health over quick gratification urges made all the difference. Think of it like this: would you rather indulge in a fleeting moment of sweetness, or would you prefer to walk into a room and turn heads? Because when you take care of your body, it's like rolling up in a shiny Rolls-Royce—everyone notices, and yes, it feels fantastic.

Now, I'm not just healthier—I'm happier. And let me tell you, being in great shape does more for your love life than any candy ever could. It's about making choices that add value to your life in the long run.

Mastering the Art of Choosing

Living at the mercy of your urges is like being tossed around at sea without a compass. Taking charge of your desires, on the other hand, is like grabbing the wheel of your very own ship. Steering towards your dreams with intention isn't just empowering; it's exhilarating. So let's make this journey fun, engaging, and filled with real, meaningful adventures. Because mastering your desires doesn't just mean surviving—it means thriving. Dive deep into your transformation with zest and zeal because what lies beneath is truly worth discovering. Are you down with OPP?

Chapter 2: Mastering the Subconscious: Tools, Toys, and Techniques

Welcome to the funhouse of self-mastery where transforming your inner world is not just necessary, it's a riot! Let's dive into how you can flip the script on old habits and script a blockbuster life with some spicy, smart, and strategic techniques.

Life Scripts: Directing Your Personal Blockbuster

Why not start with some screenplay writing? You're the star of your own life story, so let's get scriptwriting with Oscar-worthy clarity. Whether it's becoming debt-free, landing your dream job, or just being able to do ten pull-ups, write down your goals as if they're already achieved. Every morning, read this script like it's your daily affirmation—your personal pep-talk to stardom.

Cue the Visuals: Dream boarding Your Future

Imagine creating a vision board so sharp it makes reality look blurry. This isn't just about pasting pictures on a poster;

it's about constructing the blueprint of your future life. Want that new job? Visualize sitting at your new desk. Dream of a fitter you? See yourself crossing the finish line. These aren't just dreams; they're the previews of your life's coming attractions.

Winning at Willpower: The Ultimate Game

Who needs boring old self-control when you can have a blast rising above your cravings? Celebrate every little victory. Skipped the elevator and took the stairs? That's a win. Chose a salad over fries? It's about making every good choice a reason to celebrate because every single act of willpower over your body increases your manifestation power.

Mindfulness: Your Mental Reset Button

This isn't hippie stuff—it's your secret weapon. Whether you're deciding if pizza counts as a vegetable or not, mindfulness drags you back to reality, focusing on what matters here and now. Simply put, mindfulness is being in the felt presence of immediate experience. It's about training your brain to stay present, not lost in past regrets or future anxieties.

Meditation: Taming Your Inner Monkey

Meditation? More like mental gymnastics, right? Here's the real deal: starting meditation can feel less like a peaceful spa day and more like trying to teach a hyperactive monkey to sit still—frustrating, unpredictable, and kinda funny when you think about it.

But why bother? Because mastering meditation is like putting a leash on that monkey mind of yours. It's not just about silencing the endless chatter; it's about grabbing the reins and showing your thoughts who's boss. And in "Orange Peel Porn," we don't just aim for quiet—we aim for control.

Here's how I do it: I start with something simple, like staring at my finger for five minutes straight. Sounds easy? Try it. It's a hardcore stare-down with your own brain, battling out who gets to run the show. After I've nailed the five minutes, I crank it up—other hand, now set the timer for ten minutes. It's a mental workout, and yes, your brain will feel the burn.

This isn't your average, "ohm" humming, legs-crossed kind of deal. This is training your brain to sit and stay, like teaching an old dog new tricks—except the dog is your subconscious and the trick is to finally chill out. Through these exercises, you'll sharpen your focus and restore mental clarity, making you a master of your inner universe.

So, are you ready to wrangle your inner monkey? Let's make meditation the most thrilling part of your mental toolbox. After all, controlling your mind is the ultimate power play—and who doesn't want to be the boss?

Journaling and Dream Journaling: Your Subconscious's Diary

Put pen to paper and let your thoughts flow. This isn't just about recounting your day; it's about discovering patterns, solving problems, and setting plans. And when it comes to dreams, jotting them down can turn the whispers of your subconscious into shouts you can actually understand and act on. Dream journaling, in particular, is a game-changer. It's how the unusual title "Orange Peel Porn" came to me—etched in the vivid imagery of a dream. Without capturing these nighttime narratives, who knows? This book might have had a far less zesty title or may have never existed at all. By consistently recording our dreams, we not only recall them better but sometimes, they hand us gems that are too good to ignore. So keep a pen and paper at your bedside.

Transforming Discomfort into Discipline

Comfort zone? Never heard of it! Embrace challenges like waking up early for a run or facing tough conversations head-on. These moments aren't just hurdles; they're opportunities to grow stronger and more resilient, proving to yourself that you can handle anything life throws your way.

"Mastering others is strength. Mastering yourself is true power." –Lao Tzu

Manifesting Mastery: Own Your Reality

You're not just living life; you're crafting it with precision. With tools like visualization and meditation, align your daily actions with your deepest desires. It's about not just hoping for a better life but manifesting it through consistent, intentional action.

Next Stop: No More Autopilot

Ready to ditch the same old routine? Break free from the loop of sameness and start steering your life with intention and purpose. It's time to take control, make conscious choices, and direct your life towards the extraordinary.

Let's Get Real: Initiating Change, Now!

So, how do we shake things up and step off the merry-go-round of monotony? Start by implementing these tools today. Rewrite your life script each morning, meditate to clear the mental clutter, practice mindfulness to stay sharp, and journal to keep track of your subconscious trends. It's time to get intentional, get specific, and most importantly, get moving.

After all, if you don't have a plan of your own, you'll end up being a part of someone else's plan—and since yours is now authored by you, one page, one day, and one dream at a time. Let's make it a page-turner.

*"You do not rise to the level of your goals. You fall to the level of your systems." – **James Clear***

Chapter 3: The Disciplines of Speech: Words as Wands in the Magic of Manifestation

Heard of Affirmations?

Well, the belief behind affirmations is that saying things that resonate with your life will help you manifest that reality. But here's a curveball—have you ever thought about what happens when you're belting out lyrics that clash with the life you want to live? Yep, that's a problem!

Imagine this: you're jamming to tunes that go, "I'm young, dumb, and broke." Sounds catchy, right? But what you're actually doing is telling your universe, "Hey, I'm all about that broke life." Not exactly the message you want to be sending if you're working on manifesting wealth and wisdom!

And let's get real for a moment—I can listen to certain tracks, and they make me wanna dive back into habits I've worked hard to break. Drugs, bad decisions, you name it. So, I choose not to listen to that stuff because, guess what? Your body is your subconscious, and when it hears those sounds, it's like a time machine taking you back to those old feelings, desires, and urges. And I'm all about moving forward, not backward!

Speech Therapy 101: Fine-Tuning Your Inner DJ

Now, I know what you're thinking. "But I love my playlists!" And that's cool. But it's time to reassess what's on them. Music isn't just background noise; it can transport us back to our past selves, echoing old emotions and mindsets that we are working hard to evolve from.

I made a radical shift in my musical diet. I moved away from genres that anchored me to my past experiences and emotions—specifically, I swapped hip-hop and rap for instrumental jazz. This wasn't just a change in genre; it was a strategic move to support my transformation. I set specific times to listen, ensuring that what I consumed musically supported where I wanted to go, not where I'd been.

Affirmations: The Rhythm of Reality

Affirmations are potent tools, not just feel-good phrases. They sculpt our subconscious, molding our reality. If you find yourself humming tunes that underline your limitations, it's time to switch to a melody of empowerment. Craft affirmations and choose lyrics that resonate with the life you aspire to—a life where every note and word aligns with your deepest desires, creating vibrations that don't just sound good but feel profoundly real.

Crafting Your New Playlist

Your mental and emotional state can significantly benefit from this careful curation of your auditory environment. By selecting what you listen to, you take control of the narrative of your day-to-day life. Just as you wouldn't pollute your body with junk food, don't clutter your mind with music that holds you back. Opt for sounds that uplift, inspire, and move you forward.

Your Words, Your Reality

Every word you speak or hear plays a crucial role in shaping your reality. By becoming more mindful of the sounds you surround yourself with and the words you choose, you are actively crafting the fabric of your future. This isn't just about avoiding negativity; it's about actively creating a positive, empowering soundtrack for your life's journey. Let's keep the tunes supportive, the affirmations strong, and our speech disciplined. Are you ready to see how far your words can take you? Let's make every word count in the symphony of your life.

The Five Disciplines of Speech: Mastering Your Vocal Vortex

1. **Slander**: Ditch the dirt-flinging. When you sling mud, you're not just dirtying the target; you're burying your own shoes. Speak of others as if they were in the room—better yet, as if they were going to write your next job review.

2. **Gossip and Idle Conversation**: Idle chatter is like junk food for the soul—it feels good in the moment but leaves you spiritually bloated. Keep your conversations nutritious and fulfilling, feeding your mind and soul with healthier topics. Stop yourself and think before you speak. Ask yourself: Should I be the one saying this? Should I be the one saying this now? Should I be the one saying this here? By this time, the chance to put your foot in your mouth has usually passed.

3. **Abusive and Unkind Speech**: Every harsh word is a boomerang that eventually comes back to hit you. Infuse kindness into your speech, even on the worst days. It's not just about being nice; it's strategic soul-building.

4. **Frivolity or Irreverent Speech**: Sure, a little humor goes a long way, but let's keep it uplifting. Frivolous talk may seem harmless, but it often distracts from the values and visions you're trying to manifest.

5. **Critical, Captious, or Fault-finding Speech**: Constructive criticism is a tool; destructively critical speech is a weapon. Learn to wield your words with precision.

Neville Goddard and the Internal Conversations

Channeling Neville Goddard, remember that every internal dialogue is a mini-creation. Your silent words shape the universe inside you, which then influences the universe around you. This isn't just metaphysical mumbo-jumbo; it's quantum physics with a mystical twist. Match the frequency of the reality you want, and you cannot help but get that reality. This principle asserts that by aligning your internal narrative with the vibrations of your desired outcomes, you effectively tune into the possibilities and draw them closer to your experience. It's about becoming a resonant beacon for your aspirations, ensuring that your internal world vibrates in harmony with the external results you seek.

Manifesting with Every Word

By the time you turn this page, you'll not only be wary of what you say but excited to use your speech as a tool for transformation.

Words have power—the power to create and the power to destroy. Let's choose creation, shall we?

Are You Down with OPP?

As we close this chapter in "Orange Peel Porn," ask yourself if you're truly down with OPP—Owning your Personal Power. With every word spoken, sung, or thought, you're casting spells. Choose your incantations wisely, aligning your speech with the magnificent life you're destined to live. Let's not just talk the talk but walk the walk, one powerful word at a time.

Ready to change the tunes of your life's soundtrack? Let's harmonize our words with our highest intentions, turning everyday speech into everyday miracles.

Chapter 4: Embracing Solitude: Shielding Yourself from Negativity

In our quest for self-mastery, recognizing the power of our social environment is key. Just like our bodies are a billboard for our subconscious thoughts, our emotional state often reflects the emotions buzzing around us. That's why sometimes, solitude isn't just a nice little retreat—it's your strategic shield in the epic quest for personal growth.

The Contagion of Negativity

Let's face it, negativity can spread faster than gossip in a small town. Hanging around people who are chronically negative can sneakily mess with your own state of mind and emotions. It's like catching a cold, but instead of sneezes, you're catching frowns and pessimism.

And here's the kicker—I don't care if it's your own mother, if she's radiating negativity like a nuclear reactor, you might need to love her from a distance. Yep, even if she's the sweetest peach in the orchard, if she's oozing sour vibes, it's

time to step back. It's not about not loving these people —
it's about loving yourself more.

It's crucial to recognize that while we might want to be there
for others, we need to ensure we're not turning into
emotional sponges, soaking up all their gloom. This
sometimes means choosing solitude or distancing ourselves
from those energy vampires who drain our vibe. Remember,
if they're not adding to your joy, they're probably
subtracting from it.

Solitude as a Self-Care Strategy

Solitude allows us to step back and reassess our own
thoughts without the noise of external influences. It provides
the space to reflect, heal, and fortify our minds. In solitude,
we find the silence necessary to listen deeply to our inner
voice, discern our true feelings, and make decisions that
align with our deepest values.

Practical Steps to Effective Solitude

- Scheduled Time Alone: Regularly schedule periods
  of solitude. Use this time for meditation, reflection,
  or engaging in activities that replenish your spirit.

- Selective Social Interactions: Be selective about who

you spend time with. Choose relationships that support and uplift your spirits, rather than those that leave you feeling drained or negative.

- Setting Boundaries: Learn to say no. Setting clear boundaries with others, especially those prone to negativity, is not selfish but a necessary form of self-respect and love.

- Mindfulness and Awareness: Use mindfulness to stay aware of how different interactions affect your mood and energy levels. This awareness will guide you in making healthier choices about who and what you allow into your life.

Chapter 5: The Self-Mastery Manifestation Guide**

Rise and Shine: Mastering Mornings

Welcome aboard the transformation train! First stop? No, it's not Grand Central—it's the enigmatic hour of 3:30 AM. Why? Because there's a touch of magic in rising before the sun. It's not merely about waking up; it's about awakening to your potential. At 3:30 AM, the world is quieter, your mind is clearer, and your intentions can echo without the noise of daily distractions. This isn't just a challenge; it's an invitation to transcend the ordinary.

By starting your day at this hour, you're not just beating the sun in a footrace; you're making a statement to your body and mind: we run the show. So, begin not by scrolling through your phone, but by reading your life script out loud like it's your Oscar acceptance speech. This isn't merely a morning routine; it's a morning rebellion. Embrace this sacred time to align your actions with your highest intentions, and watch as the rest of the day unfolds with more purpose and clarity than ever before.

Daily Declarations: The Millionaire Mindset

Reading your declaration aloud each morning isn't just motivational; it's transformational. It embeds your ambitions into your everyday, keeping your mindset locked on your targets. Whether you're envisioning riches, relationships, or personal records, keep that script in the spotlight of your mind's eye throughout the day.

Cold Showers: The Polar Plunge of Discipline

Next up, the cold shower. It's not just about hygiene; it's about starting your day with a statement. Think of it as a polar bear dip for your soul, a literal wake-up call that chills the sleepy comfort zone right out of you. This is where you tell every lazy bone in your body, "Hey, if we can handle this, we can handle anything."

Mindful Movements: Zen and the Art of Not Hitting Snooze

Now, let's get moving—but mindfully. Stretch, do yoga, or just dance around your kitchen. The point? Keep the blood flowing and the mind glowing. Physical activity sets the tone for a dynamic day, keeping the dreary drag of inertia at bay.

Elevating Your Game with Daily Reads

Let's talk about leveling up your life, one page at a time. Reading isn't just for the bookworms; it's your secret weapon against stagnation. Think of it this way: if you're not reading, you're just as uninformed as someone who can't read. Carve out time each day to dive into books that challenge your mind and expand your horizon. It's like feeding your brain a protein shake—it gets stronger, quicker, more agile. Whether it's a chapter a day or an article that sparks your curiosity, make reading as essential as that morning cup of coffee you stopped drinking, lol. After all, a day you read is a day you grow—an absolute game-changer in the sport of life mastery!

The Power of Goal Setting: Scripting Success

Post-stretch, it's time to get strategic with some goal setting. This isn't about vague wishes; it's about concrete steps. Write down what you'll conquer today, this week, this month—heck, even this year. Setting goals is like creating a treasure map where X marks every spot you're about to hit.

Chapter 6: Digital Detox: Kicking the Social Scroll

Introduction: Breaking Free from the Digital Chains

Let's get real for a moment—social media is like that clingy friend who keeps reminding you of all the silly things you did back in high school. Sure, it's fun to reminisce now and then, but if you're trying to transform into a superhero, you don't need a daily flashback showing you as a sidekick. It's time to cut the cord on those features that tether you to the past, like Facebook's "Time Hop" and Snapchat's "Memories." If you're diving into the world of "Orange Peel Porn," the first thing you want in the morning isn't a blast from the past but a blast of fresh motivation!

Why Morning Nostalgia Isn't Always Your Friend

Every morning, right out of the gate, social media loves to hit you with a "This Day in History" of your life. While this can be sweet and sometimes eye-opening, it's often just a sneaky way to anchor your sense of self to who you were, not who you're becoming. If you're on a quest for transformation, you don't need yesterday's snapshots defining today's potential. Remember, in the journey of self-mastery, yesterday's you is just an amateur version of today's rockstar.

Curating Your Digital Experience

Here's a radical idea: what if the first thing you saw each morning was your written goals or an inspirational quote instead of a memory of that awkward party three years ago? Managing your digital environment is crucial. Keep social media, but tweak it:

1. **Disable Nostalgia Features:** Turn off those memory features. Yes, even those cute puppy videos from two years ago. Let's keep our eyes on the prize, folks!

2. **Morning Routine Swap:** Replace the morning scroll with a morning stroll or any activity that grounds you in the now and fuels your day with intention.

Navigating Emotional Memories

It's understandable—some memories, especially those involving our children or significant milestones, tug at our heartstrings. They're not all bad, of course. The trick is to choose when to engage with these memories on your own terms, rather than letting them pop up uninvited. Save the nostalgia for special occasions or scheduled reflection times. This way, you control the narrative, not your newsfeed.

Social Media as a Tool, Not a Time Capsule

If you can't cut out social media entirely, start using it more strategically. Follow pages that inspire you, join groups that align with your new goals, and use platforms to share your progress and victories, not just throwbacks. Social media should be a forward-looking tool, echoing your aspirations, not just your memories.

A New Digital Dawn

Let's make this digital detox part of your success story. You're not just avoiding FOMO; you're setting the stage for a phenomenal day, every day. By taking control of your digital inputs, you ensure that every swipe, tap, and scroll aligns with your journey of growth and greatness. So, here's to less scrolling and more conquering, less past and more future, less playback and more fast-forward. Let's turn those notifications off and turn our ambitions up. It's time to make our digital world a booster, not a buster, of our transformative journey.

The Anti-Urge: Staying the Course

Resist the morning coffee or doughnut. Every time you say no to a small temptation, you're reinforcing your mastery over more than just cravings—you're cementing your commitment to a bigger picture.

Scheduling Genius: Clockwork Precision

Craft a daily schedule that's tighter than a drum. Block out time for each activity, from your cold shower to your reading hour, and stick to it with religious fervor. This is about creating a rhythm to your day that keeps you on track and in tune with your ambitions.

Nightly Reflections: The Evening Audit

End your day by looking back at what you achieved. This isn't about patting yourself on the back or beating yourself up. It's about assessing, adjusting, and aiming higher. Reflect, write down your wins and learns, and prep for another day of domination.

Let's get off autopilot, shake off the sameness, and start every day with a clear mission: to be the master of your universe, one disciplined day at a time. Are you ready to get down with OPP—owning your personal power, that is? Let's do this, and let's make it epic!

"The greatest discovery of my generation is that a human being can alter his life by altering his attitudes." – **William James**

Chapter 7: Neville Goddard Unleashed: Supercharging Manifestation

Welcome to the Manifestation Major Leagues

Strap yourself in! We're diving into the transformative universe of Neville Goddard, the master of making dreams come true by simply insisting they're already reality. Now, hold onto your hats—because if you thought "Orange Peel Porn" was just about getting a grip on your subconscious, think again. We've been gearing up for Neville's big leagues, where the real game is played entirely in the mind.

Meet Neville: The Guru of "As If"

Neville Goddard, a.k.a. just Neville, taught that if you want to pull the rabbit out of the hat, you first have to believe the rabbit's already there. His mantra? Live in the end. This means you walk, talk, and even brew your morning coffee as if your greatest desires are current realities. Sounds trippy? Sure, but stick with us.

The Power of Coherence: Your New Superpower

Here's where "Orange Peel Porn" turns from cheeky guide to your secret weapon. By mastering your body's actions and aligning your speech with your goals, you've been charging up your coherence capacitor—Neville's turbo booster. This isn't about merely wishing for a fancy car or fat bank account; it's about having every fiber of your being vibrating at the frequency of "I've already made it!"

Manifesting with Muscle

Think of it this way: while everyone else is trying to ignite wet fireworks (a dud if there ever was one), you're launching a well-oiled, finely tuned rocket into the stratosphere. With your body, words, and mind in sync, you're not just hoping your dreams will stick—you're ensuring they manifest with the precision of a Swiss watch.

So, What's Next?

As we peel back the layers of your potential with each chapter of "Orange Peel Porn," remember: Neville's approach isn't just the cherry on top. It's the whole sundae. By now, you're not just playing the manifestation game; you're setting the rules. So, let's crank it up a notch and show the universe how it's done—Orange Peel Porn style!

Manifestation 101: Feeling is the Secret

The core of Neville's teaching is this: feeling is the secret. It's not enough to just visualize that shiny new car; you need to immerse yourself in the sensation—feel the leather steering wheel under your palms, hear the purr of the engine, and smell the new car scent as if you're sitting in it right now. With the coherence you've developed in "Orange Peel Porn," these feelings are supercharged. Your body becomes more than just flesh and bones; it's a high-powered antenna tuned to the frequency of 'already having.'

The Power of Assumption: Living in the Wish Fulfilled

Neville didn't just suggest you think about your desires; he challenged you to live them. Not occasionally, but constantly. Embody your dreams—walk, talk, and even brunch as if you're living your ideal life right now. This isn't about pretending until you make it; it's about being it until you see it. Through "Orange Peel Porn," you've been aligning every part of your being—physical actions, words, and thoughts—with your deepest desires. Now, it's time to turn up the dial and live out that alignment every single day.

Mastering the Art of Positive Mental Replays

Ever caught yourself replaying the day's lowlights in your mind's theater while lying in bed? It's like a private screening of "The Worst of Today," featuring you as the not-so-silent critic. It's easy to spiral down this path, especially when the world's quiet and there's nothing to distract your brain from its favorite blooper reel. This mental rerun does more than rob you of sleep—it imprints negativity right into your subconscious.

Here's a fun fact: wallowing in mental reruns of daily downers is like being one percent away from completely suffering from neurosis, except we know better than to narrate these thoughts out loud (hopefully). Instead of letting your brain camp out in yesterday's regrets or that cringeworthy comeback you should've said, flip the script. Engage in what Neville Goddard dubbed "revisioning"—a technique where you replay the day's events in a more positive or successful light.

Quick Revision Technique for Daily Use

Had a disagreement with your partner? Instead of replaying the argument, mentally rewrite it: see both of you understanding each other perfectly, resolving the issue, and ending with smiles. Imagine it so vividly that it feels resolved. Now, let it go. Think of this as mentally declaring "so mote it be," effectively reprogramming your response to stress. This technique isn't just make-believe; it's a proactive way to influence your emotional health and improve your interactions.

Visualization: Your Imagination Gym

Think of visualization as your imagination's workout session. You don't just casually imagine the end goal; you live it in your mind with vivid detail. Here's where your disciplined speech comes into play. Describe your visions with precision, talk about them as realities, and watch as your words start constructing your world.

Mental Diets: Feeding Your Mind Lean, Mean, Positive Thoughts

Neville talks about the importance of a mental diet—feeding your mind good thoughts only. Just as you wouldn't eat junk food while training for a marathon, don't let negative thoughts sabotage your mental fitness. Your mastery over idle and negative speech sets you up perfectly for this. No trash talk, just treasure thoughts.

Persistence Pays: The Art of Sticking with It

Here's the part that trips many up: persistence. Neville's methods require you to stick with your mental state, even when reality seems to disagree. It's like insisting it's sunny when you're getting drenched in the rain—except eventually, with enough persistence, the weather in your world changes.

Why This All Works

Bringing it all together, the reason you're going to succeed where others may falter is simple: coherence. You've aligned your body's actions, your speech's intentions, and now, your mind's creations. This triad of alignment is the golden ticket in Neville's world of manifestation.

Manifesting the Neville Way

As you wrap up this chapter and prepare to set forth, remember: Neville Goddard's teachings aren't just about changing what you think; they're about transforming who you are. You're not just learning to manifest; you're becoming a manifestor. With your body in check, your words in power, and your mind on fire, there's nothing you can't bring into reality.

Chapter 8: Bedtime Manifestation Guide: Entering Your Wish Fulfilled

Manifesting your desires doesn't have to be a complex ritual; it can be as simple and delightful as meeting a lover each night. Neville Goddard taught the powerful technique of falling asleep in the state akin to sleep (SATs), where you ease into your subconscious with a clear vision of your desired reality. Here's a concise, step-by-step guide to make every night a stepping stone to your dream life.

Step 1: Create a Relaxing Bedtime Routine

Begin by establishing a calming bedtime routine. Dim the lights, perhaps light a candle or incense, and play some soft, soothing music. The goal is to signal to your body and mind that it's time to wind down and shift towards inner peace.

Step 2: Get Comfortable and Relax Your

Body Lie down in a comfortable position, preferably on your back, and close your eyes. Take deep, slow breaths to relax your body. Consciously release tension starting from your toes and moving up to your head. With each breath, feel yourself sinking deeper into the mattress, letting go of the day's stresses.

Step 3: Enter the State Akin to Sleep (SATs)

As you feel your body relax, bring your attention to the gentle space just before deep sleep, where you're neither fully awake nor completely asleep. This twilight state is where your subconscious begins to open up, making it fertile ground for planting the seeds of your desires.

Step 4: Visualize Your Desired Reality Now,

begin to visualize your desired reality. Imagine a scene that implies the fulfillment of your wish. This could be a conversation with a loved one where you share your success, a visual of yourself in a new job, or feeling the emotions of achieving a long-held goal. Make the scene as vivid as possible—involve all your senses.

Step 5: Feel the Emotions of Your Wish

Fulfilled The key to effective manifestation is emotion. Feel the joy, pride, or love that comes with your achieved desire. Embrace these feelings as if your wish is already realized. The stronger and more real the emotions, the more potent your manifestation will be.

Step 6: Drift to Sleep While Holding Your Vision Continue to hold onto this vision and the accompanying emotions as you drift off to sleep. Let the last thoughts of the day be your life as you desire it to be, filled with achievement and satisfaction.

Step 7: Repeat Nightly Make this practice a part of your nightly routine. Consistency is crucial. Each night, as you fall asleep in the state of your wish fulfilled, you reinforce your desires to your subconscious, which begins to work on bringing them to reality.

*"If you don't like something, change it. If you can't change it, change your attitude." – **Maya Angelou***

Chapter 9: Bouncing Back Better: The Art of Handling Setbacks

Embracing the Reset Button

Let's face it, setbacks are like plot twists in your personal blockbuster—they keep things interesting, test your character, and set the stage for a dramatic comeback. Thinking of setbacks as catastrophic only feeds the drama. Instead, imagine them as reset buttons that nudge you to challenge yourself anew each day. It's about opting for the scenic route on your journey to success, where every 'wrong' turn adds depth and experience to your story.

Every Day is Draft Day

Approach each day as if it's draft day: a chance to pick your battles and choose which challenges to tackle head-on. The harder the challenge, the bigger the potential reward. It's like leveling up in a video game; the bosses get tougher, but the loot is so much better. Encourage yourself to see each sunrise as a fresh slate, teeming with opportunities to push your limits and expand your horizons.

No Bad Days, Just Good Stories

Never beat yourself up over a misstep, and definitely don't throw shade at others either. Remember, we're all human—perfectly imperfect creatures who thrive on trial and error. The more experiments you conduct in the lab of life, the richer your data bank of wisdom becomes. Embrace each setback as a key plot point in your story, one that adds richness and value to the end goal.

Cultivating Resilience

Building resilience isn't about shielding yourself from failure; it's about becoming so dynamically adaptable that setbacks barely cause a ripple in your plans. It's the mental martial art of bouncing back—turning kinetic energy from falls into motivational momentum. Equip yourself with mental agility by regularly reflecting on your responses to challenges, and adjust your strategies like a savvy general post-battle.

*"When we are no longer able to change a situation, we are challenged to change ourselves." – **Viktor E. Frankl***

The Tomorrow Mindset

Adopt what I like to call the 'Tomorrow Mindset.' When faced with setbacks, instead of wallowing in the "what-ifs" of yesterday, pivot your focus to the "I can" of tomorrow. This mindset isn't just about being optimistic; it's a strategy of proactive resilience. It's preparing to step into tomorrow with a warrior's spirit and a scholar's mind, ready to turn every setback into a set-up for a great comeback.

Mastery Through Mishaps

Handling setbacks with grace and guts transforms them from dreaded events into defining moments. They're the unexpected drills in your training program, honing you into a master of your craft. So, the next time you hit a bump, remember—it's not just a test of your endurance but an enhancement of your essence. Keep peeling back the layers, keep experimenting, and keep transforming setbacks into comebacks. Because in the grand narrative of your life, every chapter counts, and the ones with the most twists often lead to the greatest tales.

Chapter 10: The Layers Uncovered: The Proof is in the Practice

Beyond the Lab: Your Life as the Experiment

In the sprawling landscape of self-improvement and personal development, it's easy to get lost in a forest of scientific studies, each one promising the solid ground of 'evidence-based' techniques. I thought about packing this book with a hundred citations to back every claim, making it a fortress of scientific validation. But here's the kicker—no amount of scientific proof can rival the evidence provided by your own experience.

Putting Theory to the Test

This isn't a call to dismiss science—far from it. Science is a powerful tool for understanding the world. However, when it comes to the intricacies of personal growth and manifestation, the real laboratory is your life. Theories sound great on paper and even better when a study backs them up, but the true test? Implementation. Try these principles out;

apply them daily. If they revolutionize your life, that's the only proof you need. If they don't, tweak, adjust, and try again.

You Are the Evidence

Instead of waiting for another paper to confirm what works, I invite you to become your own case study. Dive into the practices outlined in this book with an open mind and a committed spirit. Track your progress, note your setbacks, and observe the transformations. This hands-on approach turns abstract theories into tangible results.

The Experiment Never Ends

Adopt the mindset of a scientist. The hypothesis? That the strategies in this book can change your life. Your mission, should you choose to accept it, is to put these theories through the rigorous testing of day-to-day living. The beautiful thing about this experiment is that it never truly ends. Each day offers new data, fresh insights, and more opportunities to refine your techniques.

*"The secret of change is to focus all of your energy not on fighting the old, but on building the new." – **Socrates***

Time and Persistence: The Unsung Heroes

Remember, developing new habits and transforming your mindset isn't an overnight feat. Conventional wisdom suggests it takes about 21 days to form a new habit, but reality isn't that neat. If you're intensely focused and committed, you might see changes faster. Conversely, if life's other demands tug at your attention, it might take longer. What's crucial is consistency and positivity. Stay mentally engaged and upbeat, even when progress seems slow.

From Skeptic to Believer

If the methods work for you, the belief in their value won't come from external validation but from your personal victories. And if you find yourself doubting, remember: every successful experiment requires repeated trials. Sometimes, the breakthrough comes only after many adjustments and persistent efforts.

Your Life, Your Proof

So, I challenge you—step into the role of both scientist and subject. Explore these ideas with curiosity and courage. Let your life be the proof of what works and what doesn't. After all, the most compelling evidence you can find is the change you experience firsthand. Let's not just read about potential—let's realize it, one personal experiment at a time.

Living Beyond the Challenge

Though our formal challenge ends here, the practices you've adopted are yours to weave into the fabric of your daily life. Let them grow and adapt with you. Maybe the mindfulness exercises have brought you tranquility, or perhaps the refined speech has enriched your relationships. These practices aren't mere tasks to check off—they are new ways to live, think, and exist.

A Continuous Cycle of Peeling

Embrace the idea that self-mastery isn't a destination but a perpetual journey. Like the never-ending layers of an orange, you can always go deeper, uncovering more zest and more vibrant insights into your potential. Each cycle of renewal reveals a brighter, more dynamic version of yourself. As part of this ongoing process, I encourage you to keep this book close. Revisit these pages often, just as I've sometimes found myself unintentionally falling asleep with my favorite books. Familiarity with these principles will deepen your understanding and make their application second nature.

Further Readings

Embarking on this transformative journey doesn't end with this book. To deepen your understanding and continue expanding your mind, here are some essential readings and resources:

• "Feeling is the Secret" by Neville Goddard: This fundamental work by Neville Goddard lays the groundwork for understanding how feelings shape our reality. It's a must-read for anyone serious about mastering the art of manifestation.

• "The Alchemy of Vision: Exploring the Depths of Heaven and Hell with William Blake and Neville Goddard" by Yours Truly: Dive into the intertwining worlds of visionary poet William Blake and mystic Neville Goddard, as explored in my own writings. This book will take you on a profound journey through metaphysical concepts and visionary experiences.

• "The Reality Revolution" by Brian Scott: Scott explores the boundaries of time and consciousness, offering practical exercises and mind-bending insights to shift your reality in profound ways.

• Josiah Brandt's YouTube Page: For those who enjoy auditory learning, Josiah Brandt vividly brings Neville Goddard's lectures to life. His clear narrations make the complex teachings of Neville accessible and engaging.

• Liz Hobby's Facebook Group: "Neville Goddard, Imaginal Acts Become Facts When We Believe": This group is a vibrant community dedicated to exploring and applying Neville Goddard's principles of manifestation. It's a space where members share experiences, offer guidance, and support each other in the journey of turning imaginal acts into reality. Engaging with groups like this can provide invaluable insights and encouragement as you continue to master the art of manifestation.

Staying Connected

"Remember, this path isn't meant to be walked alone; happiness is best when shared. Stay connected with the vibrant Neville Goddard communities on Facebook, or drop by my Instagram at @rennwrites_marketplac. Engage with fellow enthusiasts, share your triumphs, discuss your challenges, and keep the dialogue lively. Whether it's on social media, a personal blog, or over a coffee chat, your story can ignite change in others just as their insights might inspire you. Let's thrive together in this transformative adventure!"

"Be the change that you wish to see in the world." – **Mahatma Gandhi**

Final Words of Encouragement

As you continue to peel back the layers of your existence, cling to the exhilaration of discovery, the pleasure of progress, and the joy found in transformation. You've demonstrated that you can steer the course of your life, one peeled layer at a time, dictating your reality with the precision of a skilled navigator. Welcome to the vibrant reality you've sculpted with diligence, vibrant and rich with the sweet nectar of your efforts. Here's to forever changing our lives, one juicy segment at a time. Keep peeling, keep exploring, and above all, keep thriving in this beautiful adventure we call life.

Life Script Form: Crafting Your Future

Purpose:

This form helps you to visualize and articulate your ideal future, creating a detailed narrative that guides your actions and mindset towards achieving these goals.

--

Instructions:

Complete the sections below to construct your life script. Imagine you are describing your life as you wish it to be in the future. Be as specific and detailed as possible, using present tense to make it vivid and real.

Part 1: Personal Well-being

Describe your ideal state of personal health, emotional well-being, and overall life balance. Consider your physical health, mental health, hobbies, and how you manage stress.

Physical Health:

I exercise regularly, I eat healthy foods that nourish my body, and I maintain a healthy weight of [specify weight].

Mental Health:

I am mentally strong, calm, and focused. I practice mindfulness daily and feel content and at peace.

Hobbies and Leisure:

I engage in [specify hobbies] that fulfill me and bring joy and relaxation into my life.

Stress Management:

I manage stress effectively through yoga, meditation, and by maintaining a healthy work-life balance.

Part 2: Professional Life

Detail your career goals, including the type of job, the industry, your role, and where you see yourself professionally.

Job Description:

I work as a [specify job] in the [specify industry], where I contribute meaningfully to projects that excite me.

Work Environment:

My work environment is supportive, collaborative, and creatively stimulating.

Achievements:

I have achieved [specify achievements], and I am recognized as an expert in my field.

Part 3: Relationships

Describe your relationships with family, friends, and significant others, including how you interact and what makes these relationships rewarding.

Family:

I have a loving relationship with my family. We support each other in all endeavors and communicate openly.

Friends:

My friends and I share common interests and values. We meet regularly for [specify activities].

Significant Other:

If applicable, I am in a committed and supportive relationship with [describe partner], sharing mutual respect and love.

Part 4: Financial Status

Outline your financial situation, including income, savings, investments, and how you manage your finances.

Income:

I earn [specify amount] annually, which comfortably supports my lifestyle and financial goals.

Savings and Investments:

I save [specify percentage] of my income and have investments in [specify types of investments].

Financial Management:

I manage my finances wisely, with a budget that allows for saving, investing, and enjoying life.

Part 5: Personal Development

Describe what skills or knowledge you are acquiring and how you are growing personally.

Skills Development:

I am constantly learning new skills in [specify area], enhancing both my personal and professional life.

Knowledge Acquisition:

I regularly read books, attend workshops, and participate in courses related to [specify topics].

Reflection:

At the end of each month, reflect on your progress towards making this life script a reality. Note adjustments needed and reaffirm your commitment to this vision.

Monthly Reflection

Achievements this Month: _______________________

Adjustments Needed: _______________________

Reaffirmation of Goals: _______________________

*"We are what we repeatedly do. Excellence, then, is not an act, but a habit." – **Aristotle***

Worksheet: Mastering Your Environment

Purpose:

Take actionable steps to conquer laziness and maintain a clean and organized living space.

Instructions:

Complete the steps below to identify areas in your home or workspace that need organization or cleaning, outline specific tasks, and maintain these areas once they are organized.

Part 1: Identify Areas for Improvement

1. List three areas in your home or workspace that need improvement (e.g., garage, desk, closet):

Area 1: _______________________________

Area 2: _______________________________

Area 3: _______________________________

Part 2: Action Plan

For each area listed above, outline specific tasks required to organize or clean. Set a completion date for each task.

Area 1 Tasks:

Task 1: _________________ Due Date: __________

Task 2: _________________ Due Date: __________

Task 3: _________________ Due Date: __________

Area 2 Tasks:

Task 1: _________________ Due Date: __________

Task 2: _________________ Due Date: __________

Task 3: _________________ Due Date: __________

Area 3 Tasks:

Task 1: _____________________ Due Date: ___________

Task 2: _____________________ Due Date: ___________

Task 3: _____________________ Due Date: ___________

Part 3: Daily Checklist

Create a daily checklist to maintain these areas once they are organized. Check off each task daily for one week.

Weekly Maintenance Checklist:

Day 1:

[ ] Area 1

[ ] Area 2

[ ] Area 3

Day 2:

[ ] Area 1

[ ] Area 2

[ ] Area 3

Day 3:

[ ] Area 1

[ ] Area 2

[ ] Area 3

Day 4:

[ ] Area 1

[ ] Area 2

[ ] Area 3

Day 5:

[ ] Area 1

[ ] Area 2

[ ] Area 3

Day 6:

[ ] Area 1

[ ] Area 2

[ ] Area 3

Day 7:

[ ] Area 1

[ ] Area 2

[ ] Area 3

Part 4: Reflect

At the end of the week, use the space below to reflect on how maintaining these areas has impacted your mental clarity and productivity.

Reflection:

What improvements have I noticed in my mental clarity and productivity?

How has organizing these areas affected my daily routine?

____

____

____

Worksheet : Aligning Actions with Aspirations

****Purpose:****

Encourage readers to align their daily actions with their long-term goals to enhance discipline and focus.

****Instructions:****

Complete the steps below to define your long-term goals, list daily actions that contribute to these goals, and review your progress weekly.

****Part 1: Define Your Goals****

Identify three long-term goals you aim to achieve. These can be personal, professional, or related to self-improvement.

1. **Goal 1:** _______________________________

2. **Goal 2:** _______________________________

3. **Goal 3:** _______________________________

Part 2: Daily Actions

For each goal listed above, identify daily actions you can take that directly contribute to achieving these goals. This helps create a roadmap for your daily life that aligns with your aspirations.

Actions for Goal 1:

Action 1: _______________________________

Action 2: _______________________________

Action 3: _______________________________

Actions for Goal 2:

Action 1: _______________________________

Action 2: _______________________________

Action 3: _______________________________

Actions for Goal 3:

Action 1: _______________________________

Action 2: _______________________________

Action 3: _______________________________

Part 3: Weekly Review

At the end of each week, use the space below to review your progress towards these goals. Note any adjustments needed to better align your actions with your goals.

Weekly Progress Review:

Week 1:

Observations for Goal 1: ___________________________

Observations for Goal 2: ___________________________

Observations for Goal 3: ___________________________

Adjustments Needed: ___________________________

Week 2:

Observations for Goal 1: ___________________________

Observations for Goal 2: ___________________________

Observations for Goal 3: ___________________________

Adjustments Needed: ___________________________

Week 3:

Observations for Goal 1: ______________________

Observations for Goal 2: ______________________

Observations for Goal 3: ______________________

Adjustments Needed: ______________________

Week 4:

Observations for Goal 1: _______________________

Observations for Goal 2: _______________________

Observations for Goal 3: _______________________

Adjustments Needed: _______________________

Worksheet 3: The Discipline of Speech

Purpose:

This worksheet focuses on refining your speech to enhance your personal and professional relationships.

Instructions:

Complete the steps below to monitor and improve your speech patterns. This exercise will help you develop communication that is constructive and uplifting, replacing negative speech patterns with positive interactions.

Part 1: Speech Awareness

For one week, keep a daily log of instances where your speech falls into the following negative categories. This will help you become more aware of your speech habits and identify areas for improvement.

Slander: Note instances where your words may have harmed others, even if the criticism was true.

Gossip and Idle Conversation: Record moments of unnecessary or nonconstructive chatter about others.

Abusive and Unkind Speech: Identify times when your words were harsh, rude, or unkind.

Frivolity or Irreverent Speech: Recognize when your conversation was excessively trivial or not respecting the gravity of a situation.

Critical, Captious, or Fault-finding Speech: Track when you were overly critical or unnecessarily finding faults in others.

Daily Log:

Day 1:

Slander:

____

Gossip:

____

Abusive Speech:

____

Frivolity:

____

Critical Speech:

____

[Continue for each day of the week]

Part 2: Improvement Plan

Based on your daily log, develop strategies for each category of negative speech. Outline how you can replace these patterns with positive and empowering speech.

Slander Replacement Strategy:

Example: Speak of others as if they were present, focusing on positives or constructive feedback.

Gossip Replacement Strategy:

Example: Engage in discussions about ideas and events instead of people, unless it's positive.

Abusive Speech Replacement Strategy:

Example: Pause before responding in anger or irritation; express feelings without attacking.

Frivolity Replacement Strategy:

Example: Balance light-hearted talk with conversations that have substance and purpose.

Critical Speech Replacement Strategy:

Example: Focus on solutions rather than problems when discussing issues.

Part 3: Reflection

At the end of the week, reflect on the changes in your communication and how they have influenced your interactions.

Reflection Questions:

How have the changes in my speech patterns affected my relationships and conversations?

____

____

____

What have I learned about the impact of my words on others and myself?

____

____

____

What strategies were most effective in improving my speech?

____

____

____

Worksheet: Daily Declarations and Affirmations

Purpose:

Utilize the power of affirmations to reinforce positive self-image and goal orientation.

Instructions:

Complete the steps below to craft your affirmations, commit to saying them every morning, and reflect weekly on their impact.

Part 1: Craft Your Affirmations

Write down five affirmations that resonate with your personal and professional aspirations. These should be positive, present tense statements that reinforce your goals and the person you aim to become.

1. **Affirmation 1:** ___________________________

2. **Affirmation 2:** ___________________________

3. **Affirmation 3:** ___________________________

4. **Affirmation 4:** ___________________________

5. **Affirmation 5:** ___________________________

Part 2: Daily Practice

Commit to saying these affirmations every morning. Consider placing them where you can see them each day, such as on your bathroom mirror or as a note on your phone.

Daily Checklist:

[ ] Day 1: Affirmations said

[ ] Day 2: Affirmations said

[ ] Day 3: Affirmations said

[ ] Day 4: Affirmations said

[ ] Day 5: Affirmations said

[ ] Day 6: Affirmations said

[ ] Day 7: Affirmations said

Part 3: Weekly Reflections

At the end of each week, reflect on the psychological impact of these affirmations. Note any noticeable changes in your mindset or circumstances.

Week 1 Reflection:

Orange Peel Porn

Feelings Experienced: _______________________

Changes Noticed: _______________________

Week 2 Reflection:

Feelings Experienced: _______________________

Changes Noticed: _______________________

Week 3 Reflection:

Feelings Experienced: _______________________

Changes Noticed: _______________________

Mychael T Renn

Week 4 Reflection:

Feelings Experienced: _______________________

Changes Noticed: _______________________

About The Author

Mychael Renn has been delving into and challenging philosophical doctrines for the last quarter-century, not merely in theory but in practical applications that test the tenets of life itself. He is the author of "The Alchemy of Vision," where he explores the mystical realms of Heaven and Hell alongside William Blake and Neville Goddard, and "Nailed It: A Metaphysical Translation of Bible Parables," which offers new insights into timeless spiritual stories. A father to two beautiful daughters and a man of diverse professional backgrounds, Mychael crafts his works to invite readers into a world where the mystical meets the tangible. In his latest work, "Orange Peel Porn," he continues to challenge the boundaries of conventional thinking, urging readers to look beyond the surface.